The Comprehensive Wood Pellet Grill and Smoker Cookbook

Effortless, Tasty and Budget-Friendly Recipes for Perfect Smoking and Grilling

Zhane Mcgee

BBQ Recipes for Everyone

CONTENTS

BEEF

Bacon-Swiss Cheesesteak Meatloaf

Prep Time: 15 minutes

Cook Time: 2 hours

Yield: 8-10

What you need:

- 1 tablespoon canola oil

- 2 garlic cloves finely chopped.

- 1 medium onion finely chopped.

- 1 poblano chile, stemmed, seeded, and finely chopped.

- 2 pounds extra-lean ground beef

- 2 tablespoons Montreal steak seasoning

- 1 tablespoon A. Steak Sauce

- ½ pound bacon, cooked and crumbled.

- 2 cups shredded Swiss cheese.

- 1 egg, beaten.

- 2 cups breadcrumbs

- ½ cup Tiger Sauce

Steps:

1. On your stove top, heat the canola oil in a medium sauté pan over medium-high heat. Add the garlic, onion, and poblano, and sauté for 3 to 5 minutes, or until the onion is just barely translucent.

2. Supply your smoker with wood pellets and follow the manufacturer's specific start-up procedure. Preheat, with the lid closed to 225°F.

3. In a large bowl, combine the sautéed vegetables, ground beef, steak seasoning, steak sauce, bacon, Swiss cheese, egg, and breadcrumbs. Mix with your hands until well incorporated, then shape into a loaf.

4. Put the meatloaf in a cast iron skillet and place it on the grill. Insert meat thermometer inserted in the loaf reads 165°F.

5. Top with the meatloaf with the Tiger Sauce, remove from the grill, and let rest for about 10 minutes before serving.

Per serving:

Calories: 120 Cal

Fat: 2 g

Carbohydrates: 0 g

Protein: 23 g

Fiber: 0 g

London Broil

Prep Time: 20 minutes

Cook Time: 12-16 minutes

Yield: 3-4

What you need:

- 1 (1½- to 2-pound) London broil or top round steak
- ¼ cup soy sauce
- 2 tablespoons white wine
- 2 tablespoons extra-virgin olive oil
- ¼ cup chopped scallions.
- 2 tablespoons packed brown sugar.
- 2 garlic cloves, minced.
- 2 teaspoons red pepper flakes
- 1 teaspoon freshly ground black pepper.

Steps:

1. Using a meat mallet, pound the steak lightly all over on both sides to break down its fibers and tenderize. You are not trying to pound down the thickness.

2. In a medium bowl, make the marinade by combining the soy sauce, white wine, olive oil, scallions, brown sugar, garlic, red pepper flakes, and black pepper.

3. Put the steak in a shallow plastic container with a lid and pour the marinade over the meat. Cover and refrigerate for 4 hours.

4. Supply your smoker with wood pellets and follow the manufacturer's specific start-up procedure. Preheat, with the lid closed to 350°F.

5. Place the steak directly on the grill, close the lid, and smoke for 6 minutes. Flip, then smoke with the lid closed for 6 to 10 minutes more, or until a meat thermometer inserted in the meat reads 130°F for medium-rare.

6. The meat's temperature will rise by about 5 degrees while it rests.

Per serving:

Calories: 316 Cal

Fat: 3 g

Carbohydrates: 0 g

Protein: 54 g

Fiber: 0 g

French Onion Burgers

Prep Time: 35 minutes

Cook Time: 20-25 minutes

Yield: 4

What you need:

- 1-pound lean ground beef
- 1 tablespoon minced garlic
- 1 teaspoon Better Than Bouillon Beef Base
- 1 teaspoon dried chives
- 1 teaspoon freshly ground black pepper.
- 8 slices Gruyere cheese, divided.
- ½ cup soy sauce
- 1 tablespoon extra-virgin olive oil
- 1 teaspoon liquid smoke
- 3 medium onions, cut into thick slices (do not separate the rings)
- 1 loaf French bread cut into 8 slices.
- 4 slices provolone cheese

Steps:

1.   In a large bowl, mix the ground beef, minced garlic, beef base, chives, and pepper until well blended.

2.   Divide the meat mixture and shape into 8 thin burger patties.

3. Top each of 4 patties with one slice of Gruyere, then top with the remaining 4 patties to create 4 stuffed burgers.

4. Supply your smoker with wood pellets and follow the manufacturer's specific start-up procedure. Preheat, with the lid closed to 425°F.

5. Arrange the burgers directly on one side of the grill, close the lid, and smoke for 10 minutes. Flip and smoke with the lid closed for 10 to 15 minutes more, or until a meat thermometer inserted in the burgers reads 160°F. Add another Gruyere slice to the burgers during the last 5 minutes of smoking to melt.

6. Meanwhile, in a small bowl, combine the soy sauce, olive oil, and liquid smoke.

7. Arrange the onion slices on the grill and paste on both sides with the soy sauce mixture. Smoke with the lid closed for 20 minutes, flipping halfway through.

8. Lightly toast the French bread slices on the grill. Layer each of 4 slices with a burger patty, a slice of provolone cheese, and some of the smoked onions. Top each with another slice of toasted French bread. Serve immediately.

Per serving:

Calories: 704 Cal

Fat: 43 g

Carbohydrates: 28 g

Protein: 49 g

Fiber: 2 g

Beef Shoulder Clod

Prep Time: 10 minutes

Cook Time: 12-16 hours

Yield: 16-20

What you need:

- ½ cup sea salt
- ½ cup freshly ground black pepper.
- 1 tablespoon red pepper flakes
- 1 tablespoon minced garlic
- 1 tablespoon cayenne pepper
- 1 tablespoon smoked paprika.
- 1 (13- to 15-pound) beef shoulder clod

Steps:

1. Combine spices.

2. Generously apply it to the beef shoulder.

3. Supply your smoker with wood pellets and follow the manufacturer's specific start-up procedure. Preheat, with the lid closed to 250°F.

4. Put the meat on the grill grate, close the lid, and smoke for 12 to 16 hours, or until a meat thermometer inserted deeply into the beef reads 195°F. You may need to cover the clod with aluminum foil toward the end of smoking to prevent overbrowning.

5. Let the meat rest and serve.

Per serving:

Calories: 290 Cal

Fat: 22 g

Carbohydrates: 0 g

Protein: 20 g

Fiber: 0 g

Corned Beef and Cabbage

Prep Time: 30 minutes

Cook Time: 4-5 hours

Yield: 6-8

What you need:

- 1-gallon water
- 1 (3- to 4-pound) point cut corned beef brisket with pickling spice packet.
- 1 tablespoon freshly ground black pepper.
- 1 tablespoon garlic powder
- ½ cup molasses
- 1 teaspoon ground mustard
- 1 head green cabbage
- 4 tablespoons (½ stick) butter
- 2 tablespoons rendered bacon fat.
- 1 chicken bouillon cube, crushed.

Steps:

1. Refrigerate overnight, changing the water as often as you remember to do so—ideally, every 3 hours while you are awake—to soak out some of the curing salt initially added.

2. Supply your smoker with wood pellets and follow the manufacturer's specific start-up procedure. Preheat, with the lid closed to 275°F.

3. Remove the meat from the brining liquid, pat it dry, and generously rub with the black pepper and garlic powder.

4. Put the seasoned corned beef directly on the grill, fat-side up, close the lid, and grill for 2 hours. Remove from the grill when done.

5. In a small bowl, combine the molasses and ground mustard and pour half of this mixture into the bottom of a disposable aluminum pan.

6. Transfer the meat to the pan, fat-side up, and pour the remaining molasses mixture on top, spreading it evenly over the meat. Cover tightly with aluminum foil.

7. Transfer the pan to the grill, close the lid, and continue smoking the corned beef for 2 to 3 hours, or until a meat thermometer inserted in the thickest part reads 185°F.

8. Rest meat

9. Serve.

Per serving:

Calories: 295 Cal

Fat: 17 g

Carbohydrates: 19 g

Protein: 18 g

Fiber: 6 g

Cheeseburger Hand Pies

Prep Time: 35 minutes

Cook Time: 10 minutes

Yield: 6

What you need:

- ½ pound lean ground beef
- 1 tablespoon minced onion
- 1 tablespoon steak seasoning
- 1 cup cheese
- 8 slices white American cheese, divided.
- 2 (14-ounce) refrigerated prepared pizza dough sheets, divided.
- 2 eggs
- 24 hamburger dill pickle chips
- 2 tablespoons sesame seeds
- 6 slices tomato, for garnish
- Ketchup and mustard, for serving.

Steps:

1. Supply your smoker with wood pellets and follow the manufacturer's specific start-up procedure. Preheat, with the lid closed to 325°F.
2. On your stove top, in a medium sauté pan over medium-high heat, brown the ground beef for 4 to 5

minutes, or until cooked through. Add the minced onion and steak seasoning.

3. Toss in the shredded cheese blend and 2 slices of American cheese and stir until melted and fully incorporated.

4. Remove the cheeseburger mixture from the heat and set aside.

5. Make sure the dough is well chilled for easier handling. Working quickly, roll out one prepared pizza crust on parchment paper and brush with half of the egg wash.

6. Arrange the remaining 6 slices of American cheese on the dough to outline 6 hand pies.

Per serving:

Calories: 325 Cal

Fat: 21 g

Carbohydrates: 11 g

Protein: 23 g

Fiber: 0 g

Pastrami

Prep Time: 10 minutes

Cook Time: 4-5 hours

Yield: 12

What you need:

- 1-gallon water, plus ½ cup
- ½ cup packed light brown sugar.
- 1 (3- to 4-pound) point cut corned beef brisket with brine mix packet.
- 2 tablespoons freshly ground black pepper.
- ¼ cup ground coriander

Steps:

1.   Cover and refrigerate overnight, changing the water as often as you remember to do so—ideally, every 3 hours while you are awake—to soak out some of the curing salt originally added.

2.   Supply your smoker with wood pellets and follow the manufacturer's specific start-up procedure. Preheat, with the lid closed to 275°F.

3.   In a small bowl, combine the black pepper and ground coriander to form a rub.

4.   Drain the meat, pat it dry, and generously coat on all sides with the rub.

5.   Place the corned beef directly on the grill, fat-side up, close the lid, and smoke for 3 hours to 3 hours 30 minutes,

or until a meat thermometer inserted in the thickest part reads 175°F to 185°F.

6.   Add the corned beef, cover tightly with aluminum foil, and smoke on the grill with the lid closed for an additional 30 minutes to 1 hour.

7.   Remove the meat.

8.   Refrigerate

Per serving:

Calories: 123 Cal

Fat: 4 g

Carbohydrates: 3 g

Protein: 16 g

Fiber: 0 g

Smoked and Pulled Beef

Prep Time: 10 Minutes

Cook Time: 6 Hours

Yield: 6

What you need:

- 4 lb. beef sirloin tip roast
- 1/2 cup BBQ rub
- Two bottles of amber beer
- One bottle barbecues sauce

Steps:

1. Turn your wood pellet grill onto smoke setting, then trim excess fat from the steak.

2. Coat the steak with BBQ rub and let it smoke on the grill for 1 hour.

3. Continue cooking and flipping the steak for the next 3 hours. Transfer the steak to a braising vessel. Add the beers.

4. Braise the beef until tender, then transfer to a platter reserving 2 cups of cooking liquid.

5. Use a pair of forks to shred the beef and return it to the pan. Add the reserved liquid and barbecue sauce. Stir well and keep warm before serving.

6. Enjoy.

Per serving:

Calories 829

Total fat 46g

Total carbs 4g

Protein 86g

Sodium: 181mg

Wood Pellet Smoked Beef Jerky

Prep Time: 15 Minutes

Cook Time: 5 Hours

Yield: 10

What you need:

- 3 lb. sirloin steaks sliced into 1/4-inch thickness.
- 2 cups soy sauce
- 1/2 cup brown sugar
- 1 cup pineapple juice
- 2 tbsp. sriracha
- 2 tbsp. red pepper flake
- 2 tbsp. hoisin
- 2 tbsp. onion powder
- 2 tbsp. rice wine vinegar
- 2 tbsp. garlic, minced.

Steps:

1. Mix all the fixings in a Ziplock bag.

2. Seal the bag and mix until the beef is well coated.

3. Put the bag in the fridge overnight to let marinate. Remove the bag from the fridge 1 hour before cooking.

4. Startup your wood pallet grill and set it to smoke setting. You need to layout the meat on the grill with a half-inch space between them.

5. Let them cook for 5 hours while turning after every 2-1/2 hours.

6. Transfer from the grill and let cool for 30 minutes before serving.

7. Enjoy.

Per serving:

Calories 80

Total fat 1g

Total carbs 5g

Protein 14g

Sugar 5g

Sodium: 650mg

Reverse Seared Flank Steak

Prep Time: 10 Minutes

Cook Time: 10 Minutes

Yield: 2

What you need:

- 5 lb. Flank's steak
- 1 tbsp. salt
- 1/2 onion powder
- 1/4 tbsp. garlic powder
- 1/2 black pepper coarsely ground.

Steps:

1. Preheat your wood pellet grill to 225°**F.**
2. In a mixing bowl, mix salt, onion powder, garlic powder, and pepper. Generously rub the steak with the mixture.
3. Place the steaks on the preheated grill, close the lid, and let the steak cook.
4. Crank up the grill to high, then let it heat. The steak should be off the grill and tented with foil to keep it warm.
5. Once the grill is heated up to 450°F, place the steak back and grill for 3 minutes per side.
6. Remove from heat, pat with butter, and serve. Enjoy.

Per serving:

Calories 112

Total fat 5g

Total carbs 1g

Protein 16g

Sodium: 737mg

Smoked Midnight Brisket

Prep Time: 15 Minutes

Cook Time: 12 Minutes

Yield: 6

What you need:

- 1 tbsp. Worcestershire sauce
- 1 tbsp. Pit Master beef Rub
- 1 tbsp. Pit Master Chicken rub
- 1 tbsp. Pit Master Blackened Saskatchewan rub
- 5 lb. flat cut brisket
- 1 cup beef broth

Steps:

1. Rub the sauce and rubs in a mixing bowl, then rub the mixture on the meat.

2. Preheat your grill to 180°F with the lid closed for 15 minutes. You can use super smoke if you desire.

3. Place the meat on the grill and grill for 6 hours or until the internal temperature reaches 160°F.

4. Remove the meat from the grill and double wrap it with foil.

5. Add beef broth and return to grill, with the temperature increased to 225°F. Cook for 4 hours or until the internal temperature reaches 204°F.

6. Remove from grill and let rest for 30 minutes. Serve and enjoy with your favorite BBQ sauce.

Per serving:

Calories 200

Total fat 14g

Total carbs 3g

Protein 14g

Sodium: 680mg

Cocoa Crusted Grilled Flank Steak

Prep Time: 15 Minutes

Cook Time: 6 Minutes

Yield: 7

What you need:

- 1 tbsp. cocoa powder
- 2 tbsp. chili powder
- 1 tbsp. chipotle chili powder
- 1/2 tbsp. garlic powder
- 1/2 tbsp. onion powder
- 1-1/2 tbsp. brown sugar
- 1 tbsp. cumin
- 1 tbsp. smoked paprika.
- 1 tbsp. kosher salt
- 1/2 tbsp. black pepper
- Olive oil
- 4 lb. Flank steak

Steps:

1.   Whisk together cocoa, chili powder, garlic powder, onion powder, sugar, cumin, paprika, salt, and pepper in a mixing bowl.

2.   Drizzle the steak with oil, then rub with the cocoa mixture on both sides.

3.   Preheat your wood pellet grill for 15 minutes with the lid closed.

4.   Cook the meat on the grill grate for 5 minutes or until the internal temperature reaches 135°F.

5.   Remove the meat from the grill and cool for 15 minutes to allow the juices to redistribute.

6.   Slice the meat against the grain and on a sharp diagonal.

7.   Serve and enjoy.

Per serving:

Calories 420

Total fat 26g

Total carbs 21g

Protein 3g

Sugar 7g,

Fiber 8g

Sodium: 2410mg

Wood Pellet Grill Prime Rib Roast

Prep Time: 5 Minutes

Cook Time: 4 Hours

Yield: 10

What you need:

- 7 lb. bone prime rib roast
- Pit Master prime rib rub

Steps:

1. Coat the roast generously with the rub, then wrap in a plastic wrap. Let sit in the fridge for 24 hours to marinate.

2. Set the temperatures to 500°F.to to preheat with the lid closed for 15 minutes.

3. Place the rib directly on the grill fat side up and cook for 30 minutes.

4. Decrease the temperature to 300°F and cook for 4 hours or until the internal temperature is 120°F- rare, 130°F-medium rare, 140°F-medium and 150°F-well done.

5. Remove from the grill and let rest for 30 minutes, then serve and enjoy.

Per serving:

Calories 290

Total fat 23g

Total carbs 0g

Protein 19g

Sodium: 54mg

Potassium 275mg

Smoked Longhorn Cowboy Tri-Tip

Prep Time: 15 Minutes

Cook Time: 4 Hours

Yield: 7

What you need:

- 3 lb. tri-tip roast
- 1/8 cup coffee, ground
- 1/4 cup Pit Master beef rub

Steps:

1.	Preheat the grill to 180°F with the lid closed for 15 minutes.

2.	Meanwhile, rub the roast with coffee and beef rub. Place the roast on the grill grate and smoke for 3 hours.

3.	Remove the roast from the grill and double wrap it with foil. Increase the temperature to 275°F.

4.	Return the meat to the grill and cook for 90 minutes or until the internal temperature reaches 135°F.

5.	Remove from the grill, unwrap it and let rest for 10 minutes before serving.

6.	Enjoy.

Per serving:

Calories 245

Total fat 14g

Total Carbs 0g

Protein 23g

Sodium: 80mg

Wood Pellet Grill Teriyaki Beef Jerky

Prep Time: 15 Minutes

Cook Time: 5 Hours

Yield: 10

What you need:

- 3 cups soy sauce
- 2 cups brown sugar
- Three garlic cloves
- 2-inch ginger knob peeled and chopped.
- 1 tbsp. sesame oil
- 4 lb. beef, skirt steak

Steps:

1. Place all the fixings except the meat in a food processor. Pulse until well mixed.
2. Trim any extra fat from the meat and slice into 1/4-inch slices. Add the steak with the marinade into a zip lock bag and let marinate for 12-24 hours in a fridge.
3. Set the wood pellet grill to smoke and let preheat for 5 minutes.
4. Arrange the steaks on the grill, leaving a space between each. Let smoke for 5 hours.
5. Remove the steak from the grill and serve when warm.

Per serving:

Calories 80

Total fat 1g

Total Carbs 7g

Protein 11g

Sugar 6g

Sodium: 390mg

Grilled Butter Basted Rib-eye

Prep Time: 20 Minutes

Cook Time: 20 Minutes

Yield: 4

What you need:

- Two rib-eye steaks, bone-in
- Salt to taste
- Pepper to taste
- 4 tbsp. butter, unsalted

Steps:

1.   Mix steak, salt, and pepper in a Ziplock bag. Seal the bag and mix until the beef is well coated. Ensure you get as much air as possible from the Ziplock bag.

2.   Set the wood pellet grill temperature to high with a closed lid for 15 minutes. Place a cast-iron into the grill.

3.   Place the steaks on the grill's hottest spot and cook for 5 minutes with the lid closed.

4.   Open the lid and add butter to the skillet. When it is almost melted, place the steak on the skillet with the grilled side up.

5.   Cook for 5 minutes while busting the meat with butter. Close the lid and cook until the temperature is 130°F.

6.   Remove the steak from the skillet and let rest for 10 minutes before enjoying with the reserved butter.

Per serving:

Calories 745

Total fat 65g

Total Carbs 5g

Net Carbs 5g

Protein 35g

Wood Pellet Smoked Ribeye Steaks

Prep Time: 15 Minutes

Cook Time: 35 Minutes

Yield: 1

What you need:

- 2-inch-thick ribeye steaks
- Steak rub of choice

Steps:

1. Preheat your pellet grill to low smoke.

2. Sprinkle the steak with your favorite steak rub and place it on the grill. Let it smoke for 25 minutes.

3. Remove the steak from the grill and set the temperature to 400°F.

4. Return the steak to the grill and sear it for 5 minutes on each side.

5. Cook until the desired temperature is achieved; 125°F-rare, 145°F-Medium, and 165°F.-Well done.

6. Wrap the steak with foil and let rest for 10 minutes before serving. Enjoy.

Per serving:

Calories 225

Total fat 14g

Total Carbs 2g

Protein 35g

Sodium: 63mg,

Potassium 463mg

Prep Time: 10 Minutes

Cook Time: 90 Minutes

Yield: 4

What you need:

- 2 tbsp. olive oil

- 2 tbsp. java chophouse seasoning

- 3 lb. trip tip roast, fat cap, and silver skin removed.

Steps:

1.   Startup your wood pellet grill and smoker and set the temperature to 225°**F.**

2.   Rub the roast with olive oil and seasoning, then place it on the smoker rack.

3.   Smoke until the internal temperature is 140°F.

4.   Remove the tri-tip from the smoker and let rest for 10 minutes before serving. Enjoy.

Per serving:

Calories 270

Total fat 7g

Total Carbs 0g

Protein 23g

Sodium: 47mg

Potassium 289mg

Supper Beef Roast

Prep Time: 5 Minutes

Cook Time: 3 Hours

Yield: 7

What you need:

- 3-1/2 beef top round
- 3 tbsp. vegetable oil
- Prime rib rub
- 2 cups beef broth
- One russet potato peeled and sliced.
- Two carrots peeled and sliced.
- Two celery stalks, chopped.
- One onion, sliced.
- Two thyme sprigs

Steps:

1. Rub the roast with vegetable oil and place it on the roasting fat side up. Season with prime rib rub, then pours the beef broth.

2. Set the temperature to 500°F and preheat the wood pellet grill for 15 minutes with the lid closed.

3. Cook for 30 minutes or until the roast is well seared.

4. Reduce temperature to 225°F. Add the veggies and thyme and cover with foil. Cook for three more hours or until the internal temperature reaches 135°F.

5. Remove from the grill and let rest for 10 minutes. Slice against the grain and serve with vegetables and the pan drippings.

6. Enjoy.

Per serving:

Calories 697

Total fat 10g

Total Carbs 127g

Protein 34g

Sugar 14g

Fiber 22g

Sodium: 3466mg

Potassium 2329mg

Wood Pellet Grill Deli-Style Roast Beef

Prep Time: 15 Minutes

Cook Time: 4 Hours

Yield: 2

What you need:

- 4lb round-bottomed roast
- 1 tbsp. coconut oil
- 1/4 tbsp. garlic powder
- 1/4 tbsp. onion powder
- 1/4 tbsp. thyme
- 1/4 tbsp. oregano
- 1/2 tbsp. paprika
- 1/2 tbsp. salt
- 1/2 tbsp. black pepper

Steps:

1. Combine all the dry hubs to get a dry rub.
2. Roll the roast in oil, then coat with the rub.
3. Set your grill to 185°F and place the roast on the grill.
4. Smoke for 4 hours or until the internal temperature reaches 140°F.
5. Remove the roast from the grill and let rest for 10 minutes.
6. Slice thinly and serve.

Per serving:

Calories 90

Total fat 3g

Total Carbs 0g

Protein 14g

Sodium: 420mg

LAMB

Grilled Aussie Leg of Lamb

Prep Time: 30 Minutes

Cook Time: 2 Hours

Yield: 8

What you need:

• 5 lb. Aussie Boneless Leg of lamb

Smoked Paprika Rub

• 1 tbsp. raw sugar

• 1 tbsp. salt

• 1 tbsp. black pepper

• 1 tbsp. smoked paprika.

• 1 tbsp. garlic powder

• 1 tbsp. rosemary

• 1 tbsp. onion powder

• 1 tbsp. cumin

• 1/2 tbsp. cayenne pepper

Roasted Carrots

• One bunch of rainbow carrots

• Olive oil

• Salt and pepper

Steps:

1. Preheat your Pit Master to 350OF and trim any excess fat from the meat.

2. Combine the paprika rub ingredients and generously rub all over the meat.

3.   Place the lamb on the preheated Pit Master over indirect heat and smoke for 2 hours.

4.   Meanwhile, toss the carrots in oil, salt, and pepper.

5.   Add the carrots to the grill after 1 ½ hour or until the internal temperature has reached 90oF.

6.   Cook until the internal meat temperature reaches 135oF.

7.   Remove the lamb from the Pit Master and cover it with foil for 30 minutes.

8.   Once the carrots are cooked, serve with the meat and enjoy it.

Per serving:

Calories 257

Total fat 8g

Total carbs 6g

Protein 37g

Sugars 3g

Fiber 1g

Sodium 431mg

Potassium 666mg

Simple Grilled Lamb Chops

Prep Time: 10 Minutes

Cook Time: 20 Minutes

Yield: 6

What you need:

• 1/4 cup white vinegar, distilled.

• 2 tbsp. olive oil

• 2 tbsp. salt

• 1/2 tbsp. black pepper

• 1 tbsp. minced garlic

• One onion thinly sliced.

• 2 lb. lamb chops

Steps:

1. In a resealable bag, mix vinegar, oil, salt, black pepper, garlic, and sliced onions until all salt has dissolved.

2. Add the lamb and toss until evenly coated. Place in a fridge to marinate for 2 hours.

3. Preheat your Pit Master.

4. Remove the lamb from the resealable bag and leave any onion that is stuck on the meat. Use an aluminum foil to cover any exposed bone ends.

5. Grill until the desired doneness is achieved. Serve and enjoy when hot.

Per serving:

Calories 519

Total fat 48g

Total carbs 3g

Protein 25g

Sugars 8g

Fiber 4g

Sodium 861mg

Potassium 356mg

Grilled Lamb with Sugar Glaze

Prep Time: 15 Minutes

Cook Time: 20 Minutes

Yield: 4

What you need:

- 1/4 cup sugar
- 2 tbsp. ground ginger
- 2 tbsp. dried tarragon
- 1/2 tbsp. salt
- 1 tbsp. black pepper, ground
- 1 tbsp. ground cinnamon
- 1 tbsp. garlic powder
- Four lamb chops

Steps:

1. In a mixing bowl, mix sugar, ground ginger, tarragon, salt, pepper, cinnamon, and garlic.
2. Rub the lamb chops with the mixture and refrigerate for an hour.
3. Meanwhile, preheat your Pit Master.
4. Brush the grill grates with oil and place the marinated lamb chops on it—Cook for 5 minutes on each side.
5. Serve and enjoy.

Per serving:

Calories 241

Total fat 11g

Total carbs 18g

Protein 16g

Sugars 16g

Fiber 7g

Sodium 332mg

Potassium 257mg

Grilled Leg of Lamb Steak

Prep Time: 10 Minutes

Cook Time: 10 Minutes

Yield: 4

What you need:

- 4 reaches lamb steaks, bone-in
- 1/4 cup olive oil
- Four garlic cloves, minced.
- 1 tbsp. rosemary freshly chopped.
- Salt and pepper to taste

Steps:

1. Arrange the steak in a dish in a single layer. Cover the meat with oil, garlic, fresh rosemary, salt, and pepper.
2. Flip the meat to coat on all sides and let it marinate for 30 minutes.
3. Preheat your Pit Master and lightly oil the grates. Cook the meat on the grill until well browned on both sides, and the internal temperature reaches 140OF.
4. Serve and enjoy.

Per serving:

Calories 323

Total fat 29g

Total carbs 7g

Protein 26g

Sugars 1g

Fiber 2g

Sodium 111mg

Potassium 408mg

Garlic Rack Lamb

Prep Time: 45 Minutes

Cook Time: 3 Hours

Yield: 4

What you need:

- Lamb Rack
- Basil – 1 teaspoon
- Oregano – 1 teaspoon
- Peppermill – 10 cranks
- Marsala wine – 3 oz.
- Cram Sherry – 3 oz.
- Olive oil
- Madeira wine – 3 oz.
- Balsamic vinegar – 3 oz.
- Rosemary – 1 teaspoon

Steps:

1. Add all the ingredients into a zip bag the mix well to form an emulsion.

2. Place the rack lamb into the bag the release all the air as you rub the marinade all over the lamb.

3. Let it stay in the bag for about 45 minutes.

4. Get the wood pellet grill preheated to 2500F, then cook the lamb for 3 hours as you turn on both sides.

5.   Ensure that the internal temperature is at 1650F before removing from the grill.

6.   Allow to cool for a few minutes, then serve and enjoy.

Per serving:

Calories: 291 Cal

Protein: 26 g

Fat: 21 g

Braised Lamb Shank

Prep Time: 20 Minutes

Cook Time: 4 Hours

Yield: 6

What you need:

- Lamb shanks – 4

- Olive oil as required.

- Beef broth – 1 cup

- Red wine – 1 cup

- Fresh thyme and sprigs – 4

Steps:

1. Season lamb shanks with prime rib rub, then allow resting.

2. Get the wood pellet grill temperature set to high, then cook the lamb shanks for about 30 minutes.

3. Place the shanks directly on the grill grate, then cook for another 20 minutes until browned on the outside.

4. Transfer the cooked lamb shanks into a Dutch oven, then pour beef broth, the herbs, and wine. Cover it with a fitting lid, then place it back on the grill grate and allow it to cook at a reduced temperature of 3250F.

5. Brace the lamb shanks for about 3 hours or until the internal temperature gets to 1800F.

6. Remove the lid once ready, then serve on a platter together with the accumulated juices and enjoy.

Per serving:

Calories: 312 Cal

Protein: 27 g

Fat: 24 g

Simple Grilled Lamb Chops

Prep Time: 10 minutes

Cook Time: 6 minutes

Yield: 6

What you need:

- 1/4 cup distilled white vinegar.
- 2 tbsp. salt
- 1/2 tbsp. black pepper
- 1 tbsp. garlic, minced.
- 1 onion thinly sliced.
- 2 tbsp. olive oil
- 2 lb. lamb chops

Intolerances:

- Gluten-Free
- Egg-Free
- Lactose-Free

Steps:

1.   In a resealable bag, mix vinegar, salt, black pepper, garlic, sliced onion, and oil until all salt has dissolved.

2.   Add the lamb chops and toss until well coated. Place in the fridge to marinate for 2 hours.

3.   Preheat the wood pellet grill to high heat.

4.   Remove the lamb from the fridge and discard the marinade. Wrap any exposed bones with foil.

5.   Grill the lamb for 3 minutes per side. You can also broil in a broiler for more crispness.

6.   Serve and enjoy.

Per serving:

Calories: 519

Fat: 45g

Carbs: 2g

Protein: 25g

Prep Time: 20 minutes

Cook Time: 6 minutes

Yield: 10

What you need:

- 1 lb. lamb shoulder cut into 1/2-inch pieces.

- 10 skewers

- 2 tbsp. ground cumin

- 2 tbsp. red pepper flakes

- 1 tbsp. salt

Intolerances:

- Gluten-Free

- Egg-Free

- Lactose-Free

Steps:

1. Thread the lamb pieces onto skewers.

2. Preheat the wood pellet grill to medium heat and lightly oil the grill grate.

3. Place the skewers on the grill grate and cook while turning occasionally. Sprinkle cumin, pepper flakes, and salt every time you turn the skewer.

4. Cook for 6 minutes or until nicely browned. Serve and enjoy.

Per serving: Calories: 77 Fat: 5g Carbs: 2g Protein: 6g

Garlic and Rosemary Grilled Lamb Chops

Prep Time: 10 minutes

Cook Time: 20 minutes

Yield: 4

What you need:

- 2 lb. lamb loin, thick cut
- 4 garlic cloves, minced.
- 1 tbsp. rosemary leaves, fresh chopped
- 1 tbsp. kosher salt
- 1/2 tbsp. black pepper
- 1 lemon zest
- 1/4 cup olive oil

Intolerances:

- Gluten-Free
- Egg-Free
- Lactose-Free

Steps:

1. In a small mixing bowl, mix garlic, lemon zest, oil, salt, and black pepper then pour the mixture over the lamb.
2. Flip the lamb chops to make sure they are evenly coated. Place the chops in the fridge to marinate for an hour.
3. Preheat the wood pellet grill to high heat then sear the lamb for 3 minutes on each side.

4.   Reduce the heat and cook the chops for 6 minutes or until the internal temperature reaches 150 F.

5.   Remove the lamb from the grill and wrap it in a foil. Let it rest for 5 minutes before serving. Enjoy.

Per serving:

Calories: 171

Fat: 8g

Carbs: 1g

Protein: 23g

Grilled Leg of Lambs Steaks

Prep Time: 10 minutes

Cook Time: 10 minutes

Yield: 4

What you need:

- 4 lamb steaks, bone-in
- 1/4 cup olive oil
- 4 garlic cloves, minced.
- 1 tbsp. rosemary freshly chopped.
- Salt and black pepper

Intolerances:

- Gluten-Free
- Egg-Free
- Lactose-Free

Steps:

1.   Place the lamb in a shallow dish in a single layer. Top with oil, garlic cloves, rosemary, salt, and black pepper then flip the steaks to cover on both sides.

2.   Let sit for 30 minutes to marinate.

3.   Preheat the wood pellet grill to high and brush the grill grate with oil.

4.   Place the lamb steaks on the grill grate and cook until browned and the internal is slightly pink. The internal temperature should be 140 F.

5.   Let rest for 5 minutes before serving. Enjoy.

Per serving:

Calories: 325

Fat: 22g

Carbs: 2g

Protein: 30g

Grilled Lamb Loin Chops

Prep Time: 10 minutes

Cook Time: 10 minutes

Yield: 6

What you need:

- 2 tbsp. herbs de Provence
- 1-1/2 tbsp. olive oil
- 2 garlic cloves, minced.
- 2 tbsp. lemon juice
- 5 oz. lamb loin chops
- Salt and black pepper to taste

Intolerances:

- Gluten-Free
- Egg-Free
- Lactose-Free

Steps:

1. In a small mixing bowl, mix herbs de Provence, oil, garlic, and juice. Rub the mixture on the lamb chops then refrigerate for an hour.

2. Preheat the wood pellet grill to medium-high then lightly oil the grill grate.

3. Season the lamb chops with salt and black pepper.

4. Place the lamb chops on the grill and cook for 4 minutes on each side.

5. Remove the chops from the grill and place them in an aluminum covered plate. Let rest for 5 minutes before serving. Enjoy.

Per serving:

Calories: 570
Fat: 44g
Carbs: 1g
Protein: 42g

Greek-Style Roast Leg of Lamb

Prep Time: 25 Minutes

Cook Time: 1 Hour & 35 Minutes

Yield: 12 Persons

Ingredients

- 6 tbsp. extra-virgin olive oil

- 1 Leg of lamb (6 to 7 pounds), bone-in

- Juice of 2 lemons, freshly squeezed.

- Two sprigs of fresh rosemary stem discarded stripped needles.

- One sprig of fresh oregano or 1 tsp. Dried

- Eight garlic cloves

- Freshly ground black pepper & kosher salt (coarse) as required.

Steps:s

1.   Make a series of small slits within the meat using a sharp paring knife.

2.   For herb & garlic paste: Finely mince the rosemary with oregano and garlic the use of a chef's knife on a clean, giant reducing board. Alternatively, upload these substances in a meal's processor.

3.   Stuff some of the prepared paste into each of the slits on meat; ensure which you upload it into the slit the usage of any of the utensils. Next, upload the coated lamb on a rack,

preferably inner a large roasting pan. For easier smooth-up, do not forget to line the pan with aluminum foil.

4. Rub the outside of meat first with the freshly squeezed lemon juice, after which olive oil. Using a plastic wrap, cowl & refrigerate overnight.

5. The next day, dispose of the meat from the refrigerator & allow sit down at room temperature for 1/2 an hour.

6. Get rid of the plastic wrap & season the beef with pepper and salt to taste. When ready, preheat the wooden pellet's grill on Smoke for four to 5 minutes, with the lid open. Set the cooking temperature to four hundred F and near the lid.

7. Roast the lamb for half an hour. Decrease the heat to 350 F & keep cooking for an hour extra until the meat's inner temperature reflects 140 F.

8. Transfer the cooked lamb to a vast, clean slicing board & allow rest for a couple of minutes then, slice diagonally into skinny slices. Serve even as nevertheless hot and enjoy.

Per serving:

769 Calories

64g Total Fat

618mg Potassium

7g Total Carbohydrates

45g Protein

Rosemary Lamb

Prep Time: 20 Minutes

Cook Time: 3 Hours & 10 Minutes

Yield: 2 Persons

Ingredients

- One rack lamb, rib
- A bunch of fresh asparagus
- Two rosemary springs
- One dozen baby potato
- 2 tbsp. olive oil
- Pepper & salt to taste
- ½ cup butter

Steps:s

1.   Preheat the grill of your wood pellet to 225 F in advance.

2.   Get rid of the membrane from the ribs' backside, after which, drizzle on each side with olive oil; finally sprinkle with the rosemary.

3.   Combine the butter with potatoes in a deep baking dish.

4.   Place the rack of prepared ribs alongside the dish of potatoes on the grates. Smoke till the inner temperature of the meat displays a 145 degrees F for three hours. During the remaining 15 minutes of cooking, do not neglect to add asparagus to the potatoes & hold to cook until turn tender.

5.   Slice the lamb into desired portions & serve with cooked asparagus and potatoes.

Per serving:

668 Calories

57g Total Fat

665mg Potassium

17g Total Carbohydrates

3g Dietary Fiber

8g Sugars

22g Protein

Spice Marinated and Grilled Lamb Chops

Prep Time: 20 Minutes

Cook Time: 20 Minutes

Yield: 4 Persons

Ingredients

- ½ tsp. fennel seeds

- One grated Serrano chili

- One 2inch piece of ginger, finely grated.

- Four finely grated garlic cloves

- ¼ cup sour cream

- 2 tbsp. fresh lime juice

- 1 tbsp. mustard oil (optional)

- 1 tsp. dried mango powder

- 1 tsp. dried fenugreek leaves

- 1 tsp. grounded black pepper

- ½ tsp. of finely grated nutmeg

- 1 tsp. Kashmiri chili powder or paprika

- 2 tbsps. vegetable oil and more for the grill

- 12 lamb rib chops (about 2¼ pounds)

- Kosher salt mint leaves, cilantro leaves, and lemon wedges

Special Equipment

A spice mill or mortar and pestle

Steps:

1.	Toast the fennel seeds in a dry little skillet over medium warmness, often shaking, for about 45 seconds, and then let it cool. Finely fall apart them with the spice mill or with mortar and pestle. Move into a huge bowl, positioned in the chili, ginger, garlic, the sour cream, lime juice, mustard oil (if utilizing), mango powder (if utilizing), fenugreek leaves, the pepper, nutmeg, 1 tsp. stew powder and 2 tbsp. of vegetable oil and blend nicely. Season the lamb chops with salt and upload to the marinade. Cover and relax for a minimum of one hour.

2.   Let the lamb chops take a seat at room temperature for one hour before grilling. Set up the grill for medium heat and oil the grate. Grill the lamb for about three minutes for each side. Move onto a platter and let it rest for five to 10 minutes.

3.   Top the lamb with mint, cilantro, and additional chili powder.

4.   Serve it with lemon wedges.

5.   Do Ahead: The lamb can be marinated 12 hours beforehand. Keep it chilled.

Per serving:

Energy (calories): 1772 kcal

Protein: 2117 g

Fat: 877 g

Carbohydrates: 202 g

Rack of Lamb

Prep Time: 20 Minutes

Cook Time: 1 Hour & 20 Minutes

Yield: 4 Persons

Ingredients

• A rack of lamb, preferably 4 to 5 pounds

For Marinade

• One medium lemon

• Four garlic cloves, minced.

• 1 tsp. thyme

• ¼ cup balsamic vinegar

• 1 tsp. basil

• 1 tsp. each of pepper & salt

For Glaze

• 2 tbsp. soy sauce

• ¼ cup Dijon mustard

• 2 tbsp. Worcestershire sauce

• ¼ cup dry red wine

Steps:s

1. Combine the whole marinade components in a gallon-sized zip-lock bag. Once done, trim the silver skin from the lamb racks and then upload the trimmed racks into the gallon bag with the marinade; blend the pieces well & refrigerate overnight.

2.   The next day, preheat your wood pellet to three hundred F in advance. In the meantime, combine the entire glaze elements in a large-sized blending bowl.

3.   Once the glaze is mixed, and the grill is preheated, place the lamb's rack over the recent grill. Cook them for 12 to 15 minutes and then baste with the organized glaze aggregate; flip & cook the meat until the inner temperature displays somewhere between 135 to 145 degrees F, about for an hour; do not neglect to baste the beef with the glaze after each half of an hour. Once done, eliminate the meat from the grill & let sit down for a few minutes. Once done, cut the beef into favored portions; serve warm & enjoy.

Per serving:

788 Calories

62g Total Fat

204mg Cholesterol

630mg Sodium

755mg Potassium

49g Protein

Grilled Rosemary Lamb with Juicy Tomatoes

Prep Time: 10 Minutes

Cook Time: 40 Minutes

Yield: 6

Ingredients

- Lamb and Sauce
- 1 3–4lb of boneless lamb shoulder
- Kosher salt and grounded pepper
- Two chopped red onions
- One bunch of rosemary leaves
- One bunch of oregano leaves
- ¾ cup of red wine vinegar
- ¼ cup of extra virgin olive oil
- 1 cup plain whole-milk Greek yogurt
- ¼ cup of fresh lemon juice
- One grated garlic clove
- Tomatoes and Assembly
- Five beefsteak tomatoes (about 4 lb.)
- sea salt flakes grounded black pepper.
- 3 tbsp. of fresh lemon juice
- One halved red onion thinly sliced.
- extra virgin olive oil

Steps:

Lamb and Sauce

1.   Put the lamb shoulder, cut side up, on a slicing board. Use a sharp knife to separate the beef into smaller portions along its herbal seams. You should discover yourself with five or 1/2 dozen pieces of assorted sizes. Put the lamb into a tumbler baking dish and season with salt and grounded pepper.

2.   Mix the onions, rosemary leaves, and oregano leaves till finely chopped. Add the vinegar and the oil and blend till rigid purée forms. Season the marinade with salt and pepper, and then pour it over the lamb pieces. Cover and allow it to take a seat for two or three hours.

3.   Mix the yogurt, the lemon juice, and garlic in a medium bowl. Put some seasonings in the sauce with salt and pepper, then cowl and relax.

4.   Do Ahead: Lamb may be seasoned one day in advance and the sauce-eight hours ahead.

Tomatoes and Assembly

1.   Before grilling, slice the tomatoes into ½"thick rounds and put them onto a platter. Season with salt and black pepper, then drizzle with 1/2 of the lemon juice. Add onion, season with salt and pepper, drizzle the ultimate juice over, unfold rosemary sprigs, and then be placed apart.

2.   Set up the grill for medium warmness. Put the larger lamb pieces onto the grate and grill till the lowest is well brown, about five minutes. Spoon some remaining marinade

over the lamb, flip and keep grilling, turning every five minutes until the lamb is roasted in spots and well browned.

3.	After a quarter-hour greater or much less, upload the smaller pieces to the grill and comply with the same instructions. They take less time to cook. The instant-read thermometer inserted into the middle of every part must register a hundred and forty for large portions. Begin checking the smaller ones after 7 to 10 minutes. As every bit finish, circulate onto a platter, spreading on the rosemary. Let it rest for at least 20 or 30 minutes.

4.	Move the lamb onto a reducing board and add rosemary sprigs on the perimeters of the platter. Tip the platter just so gathered tomato and lamb juices pool at one cease and spoon over the tomatoes. With a pointy knife, slice the lamb into skinny portions and add onion and tomatoes: season with salt and drizzle with oil.

5.	Sprinkle with the yogurt sauce and additional virgin oil and serve.

Per serving:

Energy (calories): 311 kcal

Protein: 321 g

Fat: 173 g

Carbohydrates: 88 g

Lamb Chops (Lollipops)

Prep Time: 20 Minutes

Cook Time: 55 Minutes

Yield: 4 Persons

Ingredients

- 2 tbsp. fresh sage
- One rack of lamb
- Two garlic cloves, large, roughly chopped.
- 1 tbsp. fresh thyme
- Three sprigs of fresh rosemary, approximately 2 tbsps.
- ¼ cup olive oil
- 2 tbsp. shallots roughly chopped.
- 1 tbsp. honey
- ½ teaspoon each of course ground pepper & salt

Steps:s

1.   Using a fruitwood, preheat your smoker to 225 F in advance.

2.   Trim any silver pores and skin & excess fats from the rack of lamb.

3.   Thoroughly combine the leftover ingredients collectively (for the herb paste) in a food processor & liberally practice the paste over the rack of lamb.

4.   Place the covered lamb at the preheated smoker & cook until the rack of lamb's internal temperature displays 120 F,

for 45 minutes to 55 minutes. Remove the beef & prepare your smoker or grill for direct warmness now.

5.   Cook until brown the lamb for a few minutes on every side. Let rest for five minutes, after which, slice into person lollipops; serve warm & enjoy.

Per serving:

184 Calories

16g Total Fat

12mg of Cholesterol

75mg of Potassium

6g Total Carbohydrates

2g Protein

Seven Spice Grilled Lamb Chops with Parsley Salad

Prep Time: 3 hours

Cook Time: 1 hour

Yield: 6

Ingredients

- 1 cup plain whole-milk yogurt (not Greek)
- 1 tsp. grounded black pepper
- 1 tsp. ground coriander
- 1 tsp. ground cumin
- 1 tsp. paprika
- ½ tsp. ground cardamom
- ½ tsp. ground cinnamon
- ½ tsp. ground nutmeg
- 12 untrimmed lamb rib chops (about three lb.) patted dry.
- Kosher salt
- One thinly sliced small red onion.
- 1 cup coarsely chopped parsley
- 1 tbsp. of fresh lemon juice
- 2 tsp. sumac

Steps:

1.   Mix the yogurt, grounded black pepper, coriander, cumin, paprika, cardamom, cinnamon, and nutmeg in a big bowl.

2. Season the two facets of lamb chops with salt and add them to the bowl with marinade. Turn lamb in marinade, cowl, and kick back for at least 3 hours and no greater than 12 hours.

3. Let the lamb sit down at room temperature for one hour earlier than grilling.

4. Set up the grill for medium-high warmness. Grill the lamb, around three minutes for each aspect, and let it rest for five or 10 minutes.

5. In the meantime, blend the onion, parsley, lemon juice, and sumac with a touch of salt in a medium bowl. Serve the lamb chops with parsley salad on top.

Per serving:

Energy (calories): 284 kcal

Protein: 349 g

Fat: 184 g

Carbohydrates: 76 g

Loin Lamb Chops

Prep Time: 20 Minutes

Cook Time: 1 Hour & 20 Minutes

Yield: 6 Persons

Ingredients

• 10 to 12 Lamb loin chops

• Jeff's Original rub recipe

• Rosemary finely chopped.

- Olive oil

- Coarse kosher salt

Steps:s

1. Place the chops on a cookie sheet or cooling rack.

2. To dry brine, generously sprinkle the pinnacle of chops with salt.

3. Place in a refrigerator for an hour or two.

4. Once done, put off the coated meat from the fridge; ensure that you do not rinse the meat.

5. Prepare an infusion of olive oil and rosemary by pouring about ¼ cup of the olive oil on the pinnacle of 1 tablespoon of the chopped rosemary; set the combination apart and let sit for an hour.

6. Brush the organized aggregate on pinnacle & facets of your lamb chops.

7. Generously sprinkle the pinnacle, aspects, and bottom of chops with the rub.

8. Preheat your smoker at 225 F on oblique heat.

9. For outstanding results, ensure which you use a combination of apple and pecan for the smoke.

10. Cook the lined chops for forty to 50 minutes until the chops' internal temperature displays 138 F.

11. Let relaxation on the counter for 5 to 7 minutes, with foil tented.

12. Serve warm and enjoy.

Per serving:

652 Calories

53g Total Fat

693mg Potassium

2g Total Carbohydrates

41g Protein

POULTRY

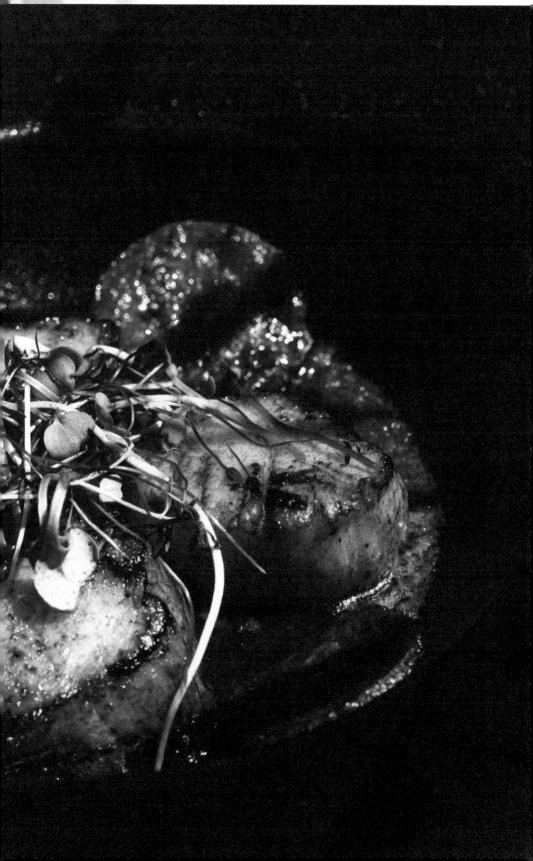

Roasted Spatchcock Turkey

Prep Time: 30 minutes

Cook Time: 3-4 hours

Yield: 4

What you need:

- 1 (18-20 Lb.) Whole Turkey
- 4 tbsps. Turkey Rub
- 1 tbsp. Jacobsen Sea Salt
- 4 Cloves Garlic, Minced
- 3 tbsps. Parsley, Chopped.
- 1 tbsp. Rosemary, Chopped.
- 2 tbsps. Thyme Leaves, Chopped
- 2 Scallions, Chopped.
- 3 tbsps. Olive Oil

Steps:

1. When ready to cook, turn temperature to High and preheat, lid closed for 15 minutes.
2. On a cutting board, mix the garlic, parsley, thyme, rosemary, and green onions. Chop the mixture until it turns into a paste. Set aside.
3. Spatchcock the turkey: With a large knife or shears, cut the bird open along the backbone on both sides, through the ribs, and remove the backbone.
4. Once the bird is open, split the breastbone to spread the bird flat, allowing it to roast evenly.

5.   With the bird's breast facing up, season the outside with half of the Turkey Rub, then follow 2/3 of the herb mixture by rubbing it into the bird. Drizzle with olive oil.

6.   Roll over the bird and then season generously with the remaining Turkey Rub.

7.   Place the turkey exactly on the grill grate and cook for 30 minutes.

8.   Turn to low temperature on the grill to 300 degrees F and continue to cook for 3-4 hours or until the internal temperature reaches 160 degrees F in the breast.

9.   The finished inside temperature should reach 165 degrees F, but it will continue to rise after the bird is totally removed it from the grill.

10.   Prepare the bird and let it rest 20-25 minutes before carving. Enjoy!

Spatchcocked Maple Brined Turkey

Prep Time: 40 minutes

Cook Time: 2-3 hours

Yield: 6

What you need:

• 1 (12-14 Lbs.) Turkey, Thawed If Frozen

• 5 Qtrs. Hot Water

• 1 1/2 Cups Kosher Salt

• 3/4 cup of Bourbon

• 1 cup of Pure Maple Syrup

- 1/2 Cup of Brown Sugar
- 1 Onion
- 3-4 Strips Orange Peel
- 3 Bay Leaves, Broken into Pieces
- 2 tbsps. Black Peppercorns
- 1 tbsp. Whole Cloves
- 3 Qtrs. Ice
- 1 cup Butter, Melted.
- Pork & Poultry Rub, As Needed
- Sprigs of Fresh Sage and Thyme, To Garnish
- Orange Wedges, Lady Apples, Or Kumquats, To Serve

Steps:

Note: Do not use kosher turkey or basting turkey for this recipe as they have already been fortified with saline.

For the Brine:

1.   In a large stockpot or container, combine the hot water, kosher salt, bourbon, 3/4 cup of the maple syrup, brown sugar, onion, bay leaves, orange peel, peppercorns, and cloves and stir until well mixed. Add the ice.

2.   Rinse or drain the turkey, inside and out, under cold running water. Remove giblets and discard or save for another use. Some turkeys come with a gravy packet as well; remove it before roasting the bird.

3.   Add the turkey to the brine and refrigerate 8 to 12 hours, or overnight—weight with an ice pack to keep the bird immerse.

4. Rinse and pat dry it with paper towels; discard the brine.

5. Spatchcock the turkey: Using a knife or shears, cut the bird open along the spine on both sides, then through the ribs and removes the backbone.

6. Once the bird is open, split the breastbone to spread the bird flat, allowing it to roast evenly.

7. Mix the melted butter and the remaining 1/4 cup of maple syrup and divide in half. Brush half of the blend on the bird and then sprinkle with Pork and Poultry Rub or the salt and black pepper.

8. Set aside the other half of the blend mixture until ready to use.

9. Prepare and ready to cook, set the temperature to 350 degrees F and preheat, lid closed for 15 minutes.

10. Roast or cook the turkey until the internal temperature in the thickest part of the breast reaches 165 degrees F, about 2-3 hours.

11. Brush with the remaining butter-maple syrup glaze while having the last 30 minutes of cooking the meat.

12. Let the turkey remain rest for 15 to 20 minutes and then garnish, if desired, with fresh herbs and or kumquats. Enjoy!

Per serving:

Energy (calories): 748 kcal
Protein: 111 g

Fat: 592 g

Carbohydrates: 501 g

Home Turkey Gravy

Prep Time: 30 minutes

Cook Time: 3-4 hours

Yield: 8

What you need:

• 4 cups Homemade Chicken Stock

• 2 Large Onions Cut Into 8th

• 4 Carrots, Rough Chop

• 4 Celery Stalks

• 8 Sprigs Thyme

• 8 Cloves Garlic, Peeled and Smashed

• 1 Turkey Neck

• 1 cup Flour

• 1 Stick Butter, Cut into About 8 Pieces

• 1 tsp. Kosher Salt

• 1 tsp. Cracked Black Pepper

Steps:

1. When all are prepared ready to cook, set the temperature to 350 degrees and preheat with the lid closed for 15 minutes.

2. In a large pan, place turkey neck, plus onion, celery, also carrot, garlic, and thyme. Please add 4 cups of chicken stock and then sprinkle with salt and pepper.

3. Put the prepped turkey on the rack into the roasting pan and place it in the wood pellet grill.

4. Cook for 3-4 hours or until the breast reaches 160 degrees F. When you remove from the grill, the turkey will continue to cook and reach a finished internal temperature of 165degrees F.

5. Rinse the drippings into a saucepan and simmer on low.

6. In a larger saucepan, combine butter and flour with a whisk stirring until golden tan. It takes about 8 minutes, stirring constantly.

7. Next, whisk the drippings into the roux and cook until it comes to a boil. Season with salt and pepper and serve hot. Enjoy!

Per serving:

Energy (calories): 621 kcal

Protein: 957 g

182%

Fat: 118 g

Carbohydrates: 182 g

Roasted Honey Bourbon Glazed Turkey

Prep Time: 40 minutes

Cook Time: 3-4 hours

Yield: 8

What you need:

• Turkey
• 1 (16-18 Lbs.) Turkey
• 1/4 Cup of Fin and Feather Rub
• Whiskey Glaze
• 1/2 cup Bourbon
• 1/2 Cup Honey
• 1/4 Cup Brown Sugar
• 3 tbsps. Apple Cider Vinegar
• 1 tbsp. Dijon Mustard
• Salt and Pepper, To Taste

Steps:

1. Prepare and ready to cook, set the temperature to 375 degrees F and preheat, lid closed for 15 minutes.

2. Truss the turkey legs together and then season the exterior of the bird and the cavity with Fin and Feather Rub.

3. Place the turkey exactly on the grill grate and cook for 20-30 minutes at 375 degrees F or until the skin begins to brown.

4. After 30 minutes, turn down the temperature to 325 degrees F and continue to cook until the inside temperature

registers 165 degrees F when an instant-read thermometer is inserted into the thickest part of the breast, about 3-4 hours.

For the Whiskey Glaze:

1.   Blend or mix all ingredients in a small saucepan and bring to a boil. Turn down the heat and simmer for 15-20 minutes or until thick enough to cover the back of a spoon. Remove from heat and set aside.

2.   Meanwhile the last ten minutes of cooking, brush the turkey's glaze while on the grill and cook until it is set, 10 minutes.

3.   Remove from grill and let it rest 10-15 minutes before carving. Enjoy!

Per serving:

Energy (calories): 333 kcal

Protein: 77 g

Fat: 22 g

Carbohydrates: 213 g

Roasted Autumn Brined Turkey Breast

Prep Time: 40 minutes

Cook Time: 3-4 hours

Yield: 6

What you need:

- 6 Cups Apple Cider
- 2 Cloves Garlic, Smashed
- 1/3 Cup Brown Sugar
- 1 tbsp. Allspice
- 1/3 cup Kosher Salt
- 3 Bay Leaves
- 4 Cups Ice Water
- 1 Turkey Breast
- 1/2 Cup Plus Two Tbsps. Unsalted Butter, Softened
- Pork and Poultry Rub

Steps:

For the Brine:

1. In a large pot or saucepan, Mix 4 cups of apple cider, the garlic cloves, brown sugar, allspice, salt, and bay leaves. Simmer on the stovetop for 5 minutes, stirring often.

2. Take off the stovetop and add in the ice water.

3. Put turkey in the brine and add water as needed until the turkey is fully submerged. Cover and refrigerate overnight.

For the Cider Glaze:

1. Let the remaining 2 cups of apple cider in a saucepan until reduced to 1/4 cup, about 30-45 minutes. Whisk in butter and cool completely.

2. After the turkey has brined overnight, drain the turkey and rinse.

3. Using your fingers, take two tablespoons of the softened butter and smear it under the breast's skin. Season the breast of the turkey with Pork & Poultry Rub.

4. When ready to cook, turn the temperature to 325 degrees F and preheat, lid closed for 15 minutes.

5. Cook turkey until it reaches an inside temperature of 160 degrees F, about 3-4 hrs. After the first 20 minutes of cooking, rub turkey with the cider glaze.

6. When the breast starts to get too dark you should cover it with foil. Let stand 30 minutes before carving. Enjoy!

Per serving:

Energy (calories): 680 kcal

Protein: 627 g

Fat: 392 g

Carbohydrates: 371 g

BBQ Chicken Breasts

Prep Time: 40 minutes

Cook Time: 15 minutes

Yield: 6

What you need:

- 4-6 Boneless and skinless Chicken Breast
- 1 half Cup of Sweet & Heat BBQ Sauce
- Salt and Pepper
- 1 tbsp. Chopped Parsley, To Garnish

Steps:

1. Put the chicken breasts and a cup of Sweet & Heat BBQ sauce in a Ziploc bag and marinate overnight.

2. Turn temperature to High and preheat, lid closed for 15 minutes.

3. Remove chicken from marinade and season with salt and pepper.

4. Place directly on the grill grate and cook for 10 minutes on each side, flipping once or until the internal temperature reaches 150 degrees F.

5. Brush remaining sauce on chicken while on the grill and continue to cook 5-10 minutes longer or until a finished internal temperature of 165 degrees F.

6. Move away from grill and let rest 5 minutes before serving. Sprinkle with chopped parsley. Enjoy!

Per serving:

Energy (calories): 183 kcal

Protein: 282 g

Fat: 48 g

Carbohydrates: 73 g

Wild Turkey Egg Rolls

Prep Time: 10 minutes

Cook Time: 55 minutes

Yield: 1

What you need:

- Corn - ½ cup
- Leftover wild turkey meat - 2 cups
- Black beans - ½ cup
- Taco seasoning - 3 tablespoon
- Water ½ cup
- Rote chilies and tomatoes - 1 can
- Egg roll wrappers- 12
- Cloves of minced garlic- 4
- 1 chopped Poblano pepper or 2 jalapeno peppers
- Chopped white onion - ½ cup.

Steps:

1. Add some olive oil to a large skillet. Heat it over medium heat on a stove.

2. Add peppers and onions. Sauté the mixture for 2-3 minutes until it turns soft.

3. Add some garlic and sauté for another 30 seconds. Add the Rote chilies and beans to the mixture. Keeping mixing the content gently. Reduce the heat and then simmer.

4.   After about 4-5 minutes, pour in the taco seasoning and 1/3 cup of water over the meat. Mix everything and coat the meat well. If you feel that it is a bit dry, you can add 2 tablespoons of water. Keep cooking until everything is heated all the way through.

5.   Remove the content from the heat and box it to store in a refrigerator. Before you stuff the mixture into the egg wrappers, it should be completely cool to avoid breaking the rolls.

6.   Place a spoonful of the cooked mixture in each wrapper and then wrap it securely and tightly. Do the same with all the wrappers.

7.   Preheat the Pit Master grill and brush it with some oil. Cook the egg rolls for 15 minutes on both sides, until the exterior is nice and crispy.

8.   Remove them from the grill and enjoy with your favorite salsa!

Per serving:

Carbohydrates: 21 g

Protein: 2 g

Fat: 2 g

Sodium: 374 mg

Cholesterol: 18 mg

BBQ Pulled Turkey Sandwiches

Prep Time: 30 minutes

Cook Time: 4 Hours

Yield: 1

What you need:

- 6 skin-on turkey thighs
- 6 split and buttered buns
- 1 ½ cups of chicken broth
- 1 cup of BBQ sauce
- Poultry rub

Steps:

1. Season the turkey thighs on both the sides with poultry rub.

2. Set the grill to preheat by pushing the temperature to 180 degrees F.

3. Arrange the turkey thighs on the grate of the grill and smoke it for 30 minutes.

4. Now transfer the thighs to an aluminum foil which is disposable and then pour the brine right around the thighs.

5. Cover it with a lid.

6. Now increase the grill, temperature to 325 degrees F and roast the thigh till the internal temperature reaches 180 degrees F.

7. Remove the foil from the grill but do not turn off the grill.

8. Let the turkey thighs cool down a little

9. Now pour the dripping and serve.

10. Remove the skin and discard it.

11. Pull the meat into shreds and return it to the foil.

12. Add 1 more cup of BBQ sauce and some more dripping.

13. Now cover the foil with lid and re-heat the turkey on the smoker for half an hour

14. Serve and enjoy.

Per serving:

Carbohydrates: 39 g

Protein: 29 g

Sodium: 15 mg

Cholesterol: 19 mg

2-pound chicken wings

• As needed Pork and Poultry rub

• Cajun shake

Steps:

1. Coat wings in Sweet rub and Cajun shake.

2. When ready to cook, set the Pit Master grill to 350F and preheat, lid closed for 15 minutes.

3. Cook for 30 minutes until skin is brown and center is juicy, and an instant-read thermometer reads at least 165F. Serve, Enjoy!

COOKING MEASUREMENTS CONVERSION CHART

VOLUME EQUIVALENTS(DRY)

US STANDARD	METRIC (APPROXIMATE)
1/8 teaspoon	0.5 mL
1/4 teaspoon	1 mL
1/2 teaspoon	2 mL
3/4 teaspoon	4 mL
1 teaspoon	5 mL
1 tablespoon	15 mL
1/4 cup	59 mL
1/2 cup	118 mL
3/4 cup	177 mL
1 cup	235 mL
2 cups	475 mL
3 cups	700 mL
4 cups	1 L

VOLUME EQUIVALENTS(LIQUID)

US STANDARD	US STANDARD (OUNCES)	METRIC (APPROXIMATE)
2 tablespoons	1 fl.oz.	30 mL
1/4 cup	2 fl.oz.	60 mL
1/2 cup	4 fl.oz.	120 mL
1 cup	8 fl.oz.	240 mL
1 1/2 cup	12 fl.oz.	355 mL
2 cups or 1 pint	16 fl.oz.	475 mL
4 cups or 1 quart	32 fl.oz.	1 L
1 gallon	128 fl.oz.	4 L

WEIGHT EQUIVALENTS

US STANDARD	METRIC (APPROXIMATE)
1 ounce	28 g
2 ounces	57 g
5 ounces	142 g
10 ounces	284 g
15 ounces	425 g
16 ounces (1 pound)	455 g
1.5 pounds	680 g
2 pounds	907 g

TEMPERATURES EQUIVALENTS

FAHRENHEIT(F)	CELSIUS(C) (APPROXIMATE)
225 °F	107 °C
250 °F	120 °C
275 °F	135 °C
300 °F	150 °C
325 °F	160 °C
350 °F	180 °C
375 °F	190 °C
400 °F	205 °C
425 °F	220 °C
450 °F	235 °C
475 °F	245 °C
500 °F	260 °C

CPSIA information can be obtained
at www.ICGtesting.com
Printed in the USA
LVHW050352210621
690717LV00009B/487